+100

Amani Saeed is a London-born Americ
Eastern-etc. spoken word artist. She is
collective The Yoniverse and has work
the BBC and the Huffington Post, amo
brings the big issues to your kitche
crisis cultivated by living between sometimes (but not always)
contradictory cultures, blurring the line between masjid and
miniskirt. Amani's poetry has been described as 'electric',
'strident', and 'brave'.

Split

Amani Saeed

Burning Eye

BurningEyeBooks
Never Knowingly
Mainstream

This edition published by Burning Eye Books 2018

www.burningeye.co.uk

@burningeyebooks

Burning Eye Books
15 West Hill, Portishead, BS20 6LG

ISBN 978-1-911570-38-7

Split

For us.

And for me.

CONTENTS

Part One

AL-FATIHAH

Bismillah Ar-Rahman Ar-Rahim:
in the name of god, the most gracious, the most merciful.

I recite these words as a heathen.
Not exactly a non-believer, not a kafir either,
but a sceptic.

I read the news and I feel sick,
pathetic, a heretic –
religion and prophetic tradition all boiled

down to demolitions and morticians.
Flag of the Islamic State waves
over the airwaves inciting hatred

and I'm left standing here
praying with the same words that they do,
bloodied hands never washed clean with wudu –

I still pray to you, oh Ar-Rahman, Ar-Rahim.
Maybe every Muslim is a part of the mujahideen,
except my jihad is about judging less and loving

more, hating less, helping more.
Deploring suicidal explosions, forced weddings,
the way FOX makes the Imam sing over images of

beheadings, drones bombarding mothers
calming their children, guarding their children,
who hope for grey skies because that means

no bombs falling today, no sirens calling today.
As silent missiles search for their prey,
instead hitting them at their play,

I think of them and pray.

But no matter how many times I say *bismillah*
I can't make the images go away,
can't make the realities change.

There are no roadside bouquets for innocent victims.
All I know is Muslim, American, we're all villains,
all sinners, there won't ever be a winner

of this war on terror
when both sides are terrorists.
One side fighting for religion,

the other fighting for money, but both
igniting the whole world, one big bomb,
every human a stick of dynamite clenched

in a palm. We invade Iraq in the name of tearing
down Saddam and install a damned
diplomatic democratic American dictator,

then watch the news popping popcorn,
ignorant spectators.
I can't find god when believing makes me a terrorist.

Can't find god
when news correspondents are careless,
can't find god when I've forgotten what Islam is.

The Imam says to pray like I can see god
but I'm clawing at my eyes because I've forgotten.
When I was small, I thought that god was Superman

without kryptonite weakness,
but now, that innocence and sweetness is gone
and god is gone too. Instead of feeling awed, I feel used:

a pawn in a universal game of chess
where I am as dispensable as the rest.
They say it's a test of your faith

and I know I'm failing hard.
Every time I hear the word *paki* it's a new scar.
People call Muslim women oppressed and burn the

Qur'an; it's no wonder I'm lost.
But I still pray.
Bismillah Ar-Rahman Ar-Rahim.

I know you can hear me,
know you're near me,
know you will make things clear for me.

I'm asking you to steer me onto the right path.
Because I want to be good. I want to be strong.
I don't want to spend my life being strung along

in this endless search for meaning
and needing to please every person –
believer or not – who tells me

I don't belong. Tells me I can't be a Muslim
and a feminist. Tells me I can't get to the bottom
of a wine glass and still press my head to a prayer mat.

My god, tell me I can be bigger than that.

Ameen.

CHAI TEA

I was told to write my own truths;
somehow, being brown is always one of them.

But I don't want to tell you
about being a 'brown girl'. I don't speak
for 'brown girls', because

like we assume white individuality, how we
separate their shades of pearl, alabaster, cream,
there are different shades of chai, coffee, and teak.

When I speak, I speak for me.
And let me tell you, I get culture shock
every time I look in the mirror.

I'm not an ABCD or a BBCD; I'm more of a
British-born, American-raised, confused as hell desi,
except I've got some other ancestry mixed

in me, but I can never be sure of what it is
because my grandma lost our copy of the family tree –
fuck me.

When god made me, he took the teabag out too early.
Omnipotent deity didn't listen to auntieji
and strained the tea leaves too quickly

when he made that fateful morning cup of chai,
tried to find a way to avoid wastage
and instead basted my skin with it.

Now I'm painted this semi-toasted tint that I can't name,
holding up a Pantone colour chart and praying
my shade's on there somewhere.

So birthed into this world with my stained skin
I'm asked the inevitable question:
Where do you really come from? As if I know.

While my brown friends call India the motherland,
I think I must be adopted—how could it be
my motherland if it didn't birth me,

if I've never seen it first-hand?
Shout-out to Salman Rushdie for teaching me
that my homeland is imaginary.

Because it really ain't my homeland, ain't even
my mother's homeland, ain't even
my mother's mother's homeland, not really.

Nanijan was taken from India at fifteen
and arranged into a marriage with a full-grown man.
Kenya the next homeland for my mother,

then Hounslow, brownsville of London,
in an attached house with pink walls where I was born
and then brought to America, homeland

number three. Now I've got this accent,
these friendships, this family that spans oceans,
ancestry that circles the whole globe.

I am proof that the whole world is home,
that this world is borderless.
There's nobody who can tell me what I am

because there's nobody who can tell me what I'm not.
I span hot desert winds and Hyderabadi biriyani,
calligraphic inscriptions and swimming competitions,

scones with clotted cream and jam
and advanced placement exams,
shalwar kameez that love my curved hips and

Abercrombie jeans that just won't sit over them,
masala dosas, samosas, mimosas, Arabic lessons,
Saturday detentions, text messages, varsity jackets,

empty Cadbury packets –
I am one international, multicultural package
wrapped up in brown paper and tied up

with white string; my song is strewn all over this earth.
So you better believe the next time
someone asks me where I really come from

I'll just tell them
I come from home.

FOR ZAK

Tonight I want to marvel at the boy
who blinks instead of cries.

He shutters his eyelids,
windshield wiper lashes stuttering.

He knows there is too much salt in this world
so he leaves the blinds open, flings

the windows wide. He can say it's just
the pollen carried by the breeze, laid in wreaths

under the memorials of his pupils that causes
them to water. He knows

there is no room for sadness
in a neighbourhood where parents split rooms and time

and when he cannot muster the shy courage to tell
the Chinese girl down the road how he feels.

He winks it away,
lets the feeling wing over his eyebrow,

whizz past his ear.
I will never know what it is to love so much

to blink away sorrow and shadow a smile
instead of leaking, to stand with back straight

as a cane thwacked over a father's palm.
To own his suffering,

hold it in his chest like
a butterfly in a jar.

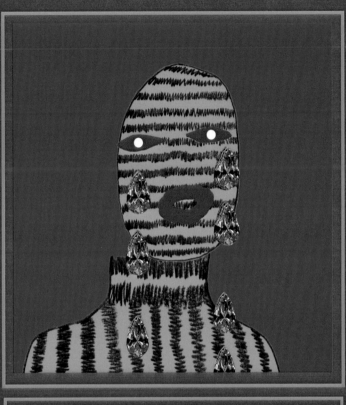

FOR ADEN

Unbury it. Let
salt spill, holy. What are we
if not flesh and blood?

THE WHITE QUESTION

Mayonnaise/cracker/redneck/pasty
Who do you lose first in a blizzard?
The white guy!

Marshmallow/Casper/vanilla/hick
What's white and fifteen inches long?
Nothing!

Damn whitey/wonder bread/gringo/paleface
Why shouldn't white people go swimming?
Because crackers go soggy when they get wet!

Privileged/racist/gora/honkie
What do you say to a white guy running with a TV?
Excuse me, sir, you dropped your receipt!

Inbred/WASP/yuppie/yank
What's white and can't get credit?
Nothing!

Pig fucker/Nazi/bleached/invisible
What's the best flat surface to iron on?
A white girl's ass!

Trailer trash/lazy/arrogant/entitled
Why can't white people play chess?
Because they've been taught that all the white pieces can be
    kings!

Fascist/skinhead/colourless

Tell me what it does to you.

EPONYMOUS

Before I was born, my father wrote out
my full name on a notepad twenty times

in careful cursive script:
A-M-A-N-I.

It means peace in Swahili,
trust in Persian;

in Arabic, it means dreams, aspirations,
something that will become true.

It is befitting of me to carry a traveller's name.
My breath is the rattle of a train,

these feet have migrated thousands
of miles, have quietly filed in queues for visas,

dipped into the warm seas of Mombasa,
fled across a partition line and tucked

themselves under car seats, paced the
dust of Indian jail cells, strode across

the mahogany floors of Iraqi libraries.
These eyes have read in Arabic,

Hindi, Urdu, Punjabi, Gujurati, Swahili, Kutchi,
English and even Spanish.

This tongue has tasted salaan perfumed
with spices, charcoal ice cream, pizza from a brick
oven in New Jersey and naan from a tandoor

in New York. I have walked the decks of ships
from Kenya to the Deccan and

I have not come all this way for you
to mispronounce my name. I have not come

this far for you to splutter over my history,
for three simple syllables to become a mystery

in your stuttering mouth.
My mother received a letter from her uncle.

Instead of signing it *regards*, he signed it
Amani. Peace. Good wishes.

When the fifth coworker today has addressed me
as *Saeed* in an e-mail chain because they can't

tell the difference between a first and a surname
I pray that I live up to my name.

When we shake hands
I'll enunciate clearly, ensure you hear

it said correctly because, let's face it,
my name is a twenty-dollar word that some people

haven't learned yet. But my name is honey.
It is aniseed, a china cup of afternoon tea,

it is the crisp fizziness of champagne and when you
inevitably choke, when your ungainly palate strains

on the richness of my name, cannot contain
three simple syllables, you expose

your crude social graces, because it's not
that my name is difficult to pronounce.

It's that you don't care about pronouncing it right.
You're uncouth. Uncultured. Cheap.

My name is Amani. Not Amina, not Amini, not
Hermione, not Marnie, not Armani, not Imani –

Amani.
Say it.

BURKINI QUEENS

Separating fact from fiction
is the most frustrating aspect of my religion.

Sometimes it's easy:
don't stand under trees because djinns

gather there in the evenings,
don't preen in the mirror at night

or you'll get possessed,
press shoulders with your neighbour

when you pray or else the Shaitan will slip in
(although if I could get the devil to pray that way

I would grace him with a space).
But sometimes

I'm hard pressed to separate culture
from scripture. My teacher once told me

that every strand of hair curling
from my hijab was a sin.

They tell me there will be more women
in hell than men.

I'm alienated by rules that I don't understand,
unsure which commands are based on Qur'an

and which are based on customs designed
to contain, constrain, make us pay for being women.

I know the reason we're supposed to dress modestly
is for our own protection, but it doesn't matter

whether we're in khimar or nothing but a bra –
men don't lower their gazes, we get catcalled

either way and if we wear any kind of veil
we become targets, get told to learn English

by crawly politicians who drawl out their racist rhetoric
over clips of refugees and immigrants.

If the way I'm dressed speaks to where I belong,
then there's not a place in the world

I can call my own. In the West I'm told to 'go
home', presumably to a land of dates, sand

and palm trees. In the East I'm asked
why I don't speak my 'mother tongue'

and I have to say my mother
never taught me my tongue,

they cut out my tongue,
I've been Englished and my whole mouth

tingles with the shame of its loss. I seek solace
in god but when I walk into my own masjid,

supposedly a sanctuary,
I still feel like a stranger.

I can't even hear the start of prayers
when I'm bustled upstairs to second-storey purdah

and they don't care about the women
enough to install a loudspeaker.

Why was I put up here?
I am not a distraction.

Whether it's god or this goddamned culture
everything I do is scrutinised, demonised, chastised.

I'll always be too whitewashed,
foreigner-coconut-BBCD-paki-cultural-mutt,

but does god reject me too?
Does not wearing loose clothing and a hijab mean

I don't respect my body?
Does walking around half-naked mean

I don't think my soul is sacred?
Is wearing a niqab licence

for a white woman to 'liberate'
my sisters and their sexuality?

As if you couldn't wear a veil
and feel like a queen?

As if you couldn't go without one
and still be a good person?

In front of god we are all naked.
I know the creator of the universe doesn't mind

if my wrists are showing
if I've shown up for prayers on time.

I may be a foreigner in every place that I go
but with god, within myself

I find home.

WEEDING

Somewhere in the desert
a man with a Kalashnikov blows into his palm

and dandelion seeds take flight on the wind of his breath,
settle over my bed. His spores thread

themselves into my dreams, split-
stitch me until I am shivering seams.

The first doubt sprouts.
It'll be enough when we're dead.

When my mother with her soft arms
has a bullet through the head

and my self-proclaimed atheist father
gets shot for his beard, when

my six-foot brother is beaten
until his newly muscled physique bleeds,

when my skinny brother's body
is strewn on the floor, wrists

that once held a tennis racket twisted beyond fixing.
Roots sink into my frontal lobe, reason

crumbling under their tight-fisted grip.
It'll be enough for the fascists when my throat is slit

and my chest is peppered with bullets
and lies. I just hope that when they come

they kill us all in the living room
when we're watching *Forrest Gump* or when

we're lingering at the dinner table over
custard and crumble because then

Al Jazeera will write think pieces
over how we integrated, how we've been here

for generations, and this
will be enough incentive for more buds to burst,

for fires to flower in thousands of minds,
the seeds scattered throughout Britain

rooted into our brains, pitting us
against these white men who call

for holocausts, these Nazis who want to *skin*
our sisters and *slice apart* our brothers until the streets run

rosy with **bloodletting** and the veins of Europe

are pure again, they will <u>rinse their streets</u>

with us and you <u>can't trust</u>

a white person, they're **devils,**

they're *war criminals,*

they're **<u>murderers,</u>** they're—

is this how we get radicalised?

By dismissing
logic as we walk
off the edges of our own tongues toward
the hateful bait dangling in front of our faces –

is this how they do it? By pitting our minds
with paranoia, filling our stomachs with rage

until our brains are dandelions
waving in the breeze, waiting to be blown?

We're a nation of inadvertent suicide bombers,
homespun soldiers conquered without guns.

As I look at my garden I wonder what I've become
and where all these weeds have sprung from.

MARTYRDOM

I don't know what to say anymore.
Everything that slips past my lips is magnified
by megaphone or microphone

and I'm ashamed. Because you think
my hand's the one that pulled the pin
out the grenade, that it's my gun spraying bullets,

my prayers slaying thousands of people the world over.
I'm ashamed because you think it's written into
my religion, you can see it on my skin:

this burden on our backs. We're the new Atlas
holding up worlds and words as they unfurl
on top of us, crush us with this weight of being

a terrorist
a monster
a Muslim.

But why is it that when white people commit
the biggest acts of terrorism we don't second-guess
them? We don't pull them aside at airports

or follow them in cars, don't tear
their headscarves off them and ask
if they eat bacon and frequent bars

knowing full well they don't. Knowing
that it's haram, but all of this sharam, this *shame* we feel
terrorises us even though we read the Qur'an

and heed the athan and pray in rows so straight
they look like the ranks of angels and raise money for
charity and practice piety and modesty and moderation

but they hate us anyway. Want to kick us back
to where they think we belong. Can't decide
whether they want to invade us or kill us

or bomb our children playing out on dusty roads
in dusty countries where no one cares
about the deaths of innocent kids

because they're not white enough to merit
prolonged attention. All we hear
are the mentions of brown men with rifles

who don't qualify as disciples of a religion
whose name is peace. They're ripe
for the evening news

and the rest of us
get the abuse for it. They never mention
that we created algebra, we invented perfume,

we had female caliphates, we watched the stars
and the moon with our telescopes centuries ago.
They don't know our past, recognise

our present, recognise that people
wear their faiths in different ways, so
if all you see is a bearded enemy or a black

mask with no face, here's a face.
Next time you read about a Muslim, think of me.
Look at my hand.

Could you picture a gun in it, pointed at you?
I'd turn it on myself before I pulled the trigger
because I love you, I respect you, I value you.

It's what I was taught by my parents, god
and the Qur'an too, and I refuse to let the few
who do harbour hatred in their hearts speak for me.

I'm staging a coup on ISIS, will redefine
what it means to be a Muslim anew.
I'm begging you to

picture me.

Try: look into my eyes.
Tell me I'd cock the pistol back
and let the bullet fly.

DEAR JO,

Listen: I don't want you to hear the machine gun
of my so-called terrorist religion when I speak,
don't want you to see just the colour of my skin
when you look at me. Look at me.

You look above me, around me, through me,
but you never look at me, never look in me,
never see me. I have always seen you as you,
not as a country, ethnicity, nationality,

but you hear my Arabic name and wonder
where my headscarf is. You ask about my traditions.
I don't know what to tell you when you ask me
what I eat at home. I eat curry same as you, roast

lamb on Sundays too, only my grandmother
adds a little extra masala because her foreign tongue
can't stand the blandness that yours does.
When you saw the ISIS beheadings

you were quick to call all Muslims
barbarians. Rest assured that I don't think
the Westboro Baptist Church represents
all Christians, that I would never use the word

barbarian to describe you. Although *barbaros* means
foreigner, and that's why you can't see me,
because I'm foreign to you.
But you're a stranger, too. I haven't yet learned

the language of hate, although slowly
I'm picking it up from you, people like you,
my religion mistranslated by news crews.
I've had to apologise for my existence since 9/11;

meanwhile you live ignorant of your privilege,
of the fact that people never have to lean in
and hear your name pronounced twice.
You are every person I have had to justify

myself to for the crime of being born brown
in Britain, for drinking and still calling myself
a Muslim. And yet I have never asked
how you could be a Christian –

let alone a good one –
for looking down on me,
for ignoring me every time I called out
your ignorance, for judging me so easily

despite the fact that your god,
your Jesus, never judged you.
Do you know me now? Am I still an other,
some exotic, unpatriotic, generic philistine,

some monster who's out to ruin
your pristine, Christian country?
Am I human yet?
Or do you need more time to define me,

safely cage me in binaries, language and lies?
I've only got one question I need an answer to:
why can I explain to you the concept of the Trinity
when you didn't even know I believed

in the same prophets, the same divinities? I'm tired
of being slandered by your double standards.
Don't shake a copy of the Bible in my face, don't tell me I
will burn in hell when you are already consumed

by the flames of your ignorance here on Earth.
Look over Matthew 23; it's a warning against hypocrisy,
talks about the Pharisees,
how everything they do is done for people to see,

that they do not practise what they preach.
So I'll pray for you. I hope one day our god
opens your ears and eyes and that you find truth.

And I forgive you.

CHARLIE HEBDO

They said
you can be anything you want
and you wanted to be an artist.

Watching white men paint white women,
rendering flesh fat and whole,
you wanted it,

wanted to be a white god,
fingers sketching little people
with big purpose.

But when you grew up
you found out they were lying
because the world tells you

what you are and you fight it
your whole life and in the end
you aren't what you want.

You yearn for the geometric beauty
of a minaret, but
there are no floating arabesque arches,

just French marches against people
who don't know you,
don't know your religion, your position

between the terrorists and the infidels.
You both play god,
creating and erasing people.

While the French tout their liberté
all you can feel are the scars
where they coloured your skin in.

Egalitarian pens left marks
as they darkened you, as they spat
on you, as they stamped

you down to what you are.
I'm not so caught up in the pretty lie
that speech is free

because while furore ignites
over the death of white men, I ask,
what about the veiled women? The brown women?

Women clad from head to toes,
shrivelled fraternité of politicians sniffing
their noses at the imminent immigrants.

Women with cinnamon skin and accents thick
with Arabic. Women whose black attire inspires
fear in the hearts of grotesque old men

who probably dream orientalist dreams of bedding
creatures like them, a personal harem
for the imperialist imagination.

But they can't stomach their spice
and slice their chadoors from head to foot,
glower over them with dirty looks, claim

they're oppressed while they seek to wrest
away the shreds of free speech that cover
their heads. There is no freedom for them.

No condemnation of the fact that their bodies
have been legislated, criminalised, regulated.
Same in Iran, Pakistan, they're all pointing

at the Qur'an and fingering at the fabric
of these girls. O, pretty girls, sinning girls,
get back under your veils

because at least if you're spinning sin
under there no one can see you,
although you'll never truly be hidden.

They'll spit on you, throw
beer bottles at you, won't let you be you
because they're all out to police you, control you.

Doesn't matter whether
they're brown, white, Arab, French, they're all
out to terrorise you,

fundamentalists and government both
hypocrites, and you will never win.
You're caught in the crossfire,

right in the thick of it.
Guns and pencils, they stencil the image
of the stereotypical Muslim on TV,

soundbites of gunshots and screams,
your body is obscene –
don't believe the bullshit they show you on the screen.

Believe in radical love.
Believe the Qur'an when it tells you,
Whoever kills a soul – it is as if he had slain mankind entirely.

*And whoever saves one – it is as if he had saved mankind
entirely.*
So I am here
with the truth

to save your life.

Part Two

THE HYMEN THIEVES

after Sharon Olds

How do they do it, the hymen thieves who
split without asking? Slick as steel knives,

poring over bodies like surgeons in
a waiting room, hands poised pincers

ready to collect cobwebs of skin.
Tender as fingertips resting on

the stem of a wineglass, as a fisherwoman
with a pink oyster in her palm, they crack open

the halves to suck triumphant from that sacred
salt centre. How do they come to the god,

to the flower still in its bud,
and prise its shy lips apart? How do they sacrifice

that virgin on the steaming altar,
watch her melt on the pyre?

They do not mistake this offering for
their own pleasure; they are like astronomers:

they know they are alone with the stellar static,
the cold ring of the telescope pressed to an eye –

just factors, like the girl burning on the bed, and not
the truth, which is

the shredded blossom, drenched
in its own blood.

FOR ALEX

It's been fifteen months
and I still feel the bruises
where you discoloured me,

the grips around my wrists
where your fingertips dug
in, the nails that left marks on hips.

I remember the feeling of your lips
on my ribs: just seventeen, I was so timid.
Forcing your lips on mine, I thought that was a kiss.

Ripping down the zip of my dress, I thought
that was passion. You said
I want you and it was an order, a command,

hands pinioning me to mattress, fingers
closing around my throat. I couldn't say no.
You ripped into me until you exposed

bone, drilled into my chrysalis skin
like an infection, siphoned away
the sweetness I kept safe inside my butterfly body.

You replaced me with a skeleton,
marrow sucked out, left hollow.
Now, looking in the mirror,

I still see your eyes reflected in mine,
you flood from my irises in rivers,
crack my chest as you fracture me,

bones start to splinter, muscles quiver
under your weight, involuntary animal whimpers,
but your hand clamps over my mouth

and I can't say
anything. Was this love?
The merest suggestion of affection,

confessions/questions/connections/contraception/
addiction/erection/dejection/aggression/obsession/
pay/attention/ignore/your/dissatisfaction/disillusioned.

These bruises are more than just marks on my skin.
They're the doors where you knocked
and knocked, tried to enter

but I won't let you come in anymore.
I can't forget. I can't forget what it felt like
to hold your hand.

I can't forget the first time we kissed,
the first time you undressed me. I felt safer
in your violence, in the easy lies you told me.

I love you, you said, and I believed you.
I had to. What else could explain
away the things you'd do, the way

you'd threaten to hit me and then pretend
that everything was fine? Then follow it with
kiss after kiss, emptiness, bliss, until I was sick

of kisses and sick of you and sick of being used.
You asked, *Are you mine?* and I said yes,
let you touch me, the thought of saying *no*

more unpleasant than the reality
of letting you fuck me. You stole
my separateness from me.

Forced me to split my body. Sucked
away at my vitality until I was raw and empty.
Although I remember your lips

and the way they whispered
along my neck, I'm taking off your kisses
and letting them slip down the sink.

I'm washing my fingers of your fingers.
I'm scrubbing your grip off the bottom of my shoes.
Whose am I?   I am

mine.
I know, now.
It wasn't my fault.

TRIPLE POINT

I used to be
I used to be
I used to be
                    fluorescent.

Neon sign eyes loud enough
to make passers-by stop and stare.
The pink
streamed off my nails
                    my hair
                    my skin,
molecules bounced
                        electric
                                down
            the corridors
                            of my halogen
                    veins

            self-supplied voltage
            to set myself alight.

            I was bright.
But that only whet your catastrophic appetite
and like a child you grabbed at the
brittle pretty light and snapped me,
neon sign turned glow stick,
quick-flick-of-the-wrist-thick-hit-of-a-brick,
            smashed glass
trickling in silver streams
                    down on the floor
as my phosphorescent essence
streamed up like gore, like atomised blood
into your hands for you to can and command.

You made me do your dungy grubby gungy dances
until I fell spent on mattresses and you
fell asleep beside me. Trapped in your chokehold,

I twisted until I could slip out of your grip,

but I had to slip out of my skin to do it.
They told me I was strong enough to

'get   out   of   it'
                but

they never told me
I had to break my own bones to do it.

Now I feel like a champagne bottle whose
cork has been
                popped,
fizz spritzing down my body in laughing, crying drops.
There is so much heaviness here.
I ache as golden tears gleam in my hair
and acid replaces the air in my lungs, soft-
spoken prayers burst midair like bubbles.

I am a surprise party gone wrong,
the VIP that couldn't be bothered to show up
because instead of hollering
and jollying at my triumph, instead
of feeling defiant, neon sign shining bright again,
all I want is

silence.

I'm tired.

I want to be soft,
pliant, ten again.

QUANTUM ENTANGLEMENT

You and I synchronise in perpendicular universes.
You flip heads, I get tails. You proceed calmly,
forgetting me, and I become frenetic thunder
and lightning, blades of light slicing
the ground where I stand.
I can't unwrite you.

As your million possible worlds expand,
mine shrinks down to the remnant
of your scalding hand
printed on
my throat.

You live in fast-forwards, we exist
in rewinds, but I'm stuck
in the middle floating

down time in a boat
that has no safety lines or anchor,
yet somehow I'm safe here.
Shielded in this moment that

                              plunges

                 off the temporal spectrum

                 and wreaks havoc

                 on the space-time continuum.

Collapsed mass tears apart
the cosmos and creates an event horizon

which starts in the light
that you stole from my eyes
and blasts through my body;

shock waves leave a black
hole burning in the cavity
where I used to be.

If anyone ever loves me again
I'll suck them up.

Gravitational hugs turned into
skull-crushing kisses,

love measured out
in metres per squared second.

That poor astronaut miscalculated
the force of this emptiness.

His arms and legs twist,
redshifted body dimming as he swims
toward the central singularity

swept

up

with captured golden dust all

swirling into
blackness.

I keep the opal bones to bury
inside of me. Because that's what I am, a
tombstone.

A void that's never satisfied,
continually craving celestial bodies
to fill the infinite hunger of the abyss,

and in the end

always eats itself

whole.

DARKROOM

I let it eat me.
I let it throw my legs back
and push me on the mattress
and suck me like
a strawberry heart. I let it slurp
my mind from
the soup bowl of my skull,
carve X-Acto tangrams
into my chest.
It harvests my organs,
uses my blood as glaze,
bakes them in a kiln,
displays them in the local gallery.
It straps me to photo paper,
exposes me naked to the light,
waves its hands magician-like
over my spine
(it never showed in the print).
It dips me in silver nitrate,
stop, fix,
rinses me gasping under tap water,
leaves me open-limbed
in the sink.
It hangs me pegged by my feet,
arms dangling like radio antennas
flipped upside-down,
signal shooting blank bulletins,
hair broadcasting at thirty-five hertz.
It slits my jugular with a penknife,
let me drip dry onto
the darkroom floor,
footprints tracking sticky
through blackened blood.

NIGHT TERRORS

These days I'm asking for it, begging.
Throwing my want in their faces
like a pair of balled-up panties,
like a fist.

Who would have thought
that being forced would have
unfrozen me, made me so
hungry?

I let them enter me like animals
and swing the trap door shut.
I want to use them up,
drain them, take

their teeth-cleaned bones
and plug up the hole
which has voided itself into me.
Every morning

I bring myself back from
the dead. I can regenerate
the skin I pull from my fingers
like peel from a clementine.

I reach for her, sometimes,
the one with the short-lopped hair
and pink corduroy jacket
who still harbours softness

in her eyes,
the one I sacrificed so young.
But now those eyes are full
of something Mother

can't recognise.
I finally understand, I've grown
my wings
inside this chrome chrysalis,

no more childish bobs, my hair
is a noose falling down my back.
I have cut my teeth on swords,
forged myself. I have become.

Since I have learned the monsters' tricks
I walk unafraid (now
that I am one of them,
could they ever really hurt me again?).

SPLIT

This is bliss.
My body weighed down on the mattress,

stones in my pockets, untensed. Sleepy.
Eyes drifting open from underwater glaze,

watching your face shudder as I half-doze,
succumb. Allow.

The feeling of you rubbing against my cervix,
gentle pinches up my insides.

As my head flops to one side, I see a woman
through the window pouring herself a glass

of wine, burgundy spilling over the brim.
Your fingers snap around my throat,

focus me into your eyes, into the sweat
pearling over your lids.

This is love. I have never felt so close
and as I step off the cliff into sleep, the feeling

of you rings into me, echoes through all my corners,
my body rising like a balloon cut from its string.

FOR AINSLEY

after the Henry Pether painting York Watergate and the
Adelphi from the River, London, by Moonlight

We could have kissed here.
Daubed in pearl, boats
rocking in the docks, cradled by black water.

No crickets sang that night but there must have
been some small orchestra, the way the water
murmured, the way the wind blew so softly

in the sails of the ships, the way
the whole world seemed to sway
as you held me.

We could have kissed here.
We could have walked along the river
and wondered how many dead bodies

were in the Thames at any given time. You could
have told me you wouldn't save me if I fell in
because you didn't know how to swim.

We could have sat on the stairs anyway,
feet daring the waves from the wall, surrounded
by crumbling brick and the snores of fishermen,

the wet whip of skipping stones across the water,
the gentle thunking of wood on wood
as the waves bundled the boats into each other.

You could have cupped my face between forefinger
and thumb, had all of London converge
around your mouth, the city melting into wet paint and light.

You could have claimed me at the Adelphi
or the South Bank or Tower Bridge
or on the glass bar overlooking St Paul's, you could

have pointed north and told me that you thought
the Barbican was ugly, we could
have talked about architecture and utopia

and I could have made you laugh.
I could have made you fall in love
in that pearl grey light, with the boats bumping

together clumsy, like kisses with eyes closed,
with the water shimmering and whispering siren calls,
with all of London stopping for a minute,
holding its breath

as you lifted my face to yours.

GHOSTS

I can escape whenever I want to, you insist.
Your hair curls in cotton candy twists
over the pillow. My fingers twitch over
your bare wrists, digits digging into the bone.

Your hands are splayed
open in pretend surrender, oval palms smiling,
and suddenly you melt into the sheets and I feel
ghost hands close over mine. Mine.

I'm sprawled over the mattress now.
Heavy hips rub white into my pelvis,
nipples minefields, throat a no-man's land.
He's got me again,

lips roam slowly over my chest.
I pray. My eyes close.
His pearl body dances rage above mine,
bonedeep graveyard rhythms.

I'll never know whether he finished.
Whether he drove it home, fell
woozy on top of me for a moment
before following me into sleep.

You surface from the sheets and
I'm unpossessed again, pinioning you to the bed.
You think you can escape
whenever you want to, but
I know better.

TO THE END, THEY REMAIN

for Denise

They shall grow not old, as we that are left grow old.
Age shall not weary them, nor the years condemn.
At the going down of the sun and in the morning
We will remember them.

I feel like a soldier on leave from a never-ending war. You, my love, are the hospital doctor, but instead of setting bones to mend, you're combing your hands through my hair, massaging tired skin.

You remind me of all the kindness I had forgotten in battle. I can't calculate the number of times he lay on me late at night while the rest of the prison guards averted their gazes, but your eyes nurse softness instead of a trip switch libido.

In my head this can only be temporary. There will never be a true ceasefire or peace treaty, chaos is sure to follow, words sure to fire, barbed-wire grips and occupied bodies, chokehold around my neck, fingers nooses, words a rope. I don't believe anything good happens without equal travesty. He taught me I earned the bruises he inflicted on me; there is no unlearning that.

We are not dead yet. We grow old as you that are left grow old. Age wearies us as it stacks up year by year, the years piled up do condemn. At the going down of the sun and in the morning, every morning, we remember them. Again and again and again, the men who did this to us, we remember them.

I ask you to remember us. Remember the girls at work with bruises and fragile eyes. Remember the shopkeepers with too-ample scarves and crackling smiles. Remember the mother who tries to shield her child from remembering and repeating brutal love, remember the strangled, scrabbling voices on telephones to helplines.

And when you have remembered us, ask why the rest of the world forgets and fails to condemn a war crime. Fails to honour our veterans, especially the ones who have been fighting the wars we could not see.

Please, remember me.

MAMA

You should have warned me.

You should have told me
that they like to wrap their fingers around
your neck so they can feel how big

their hands are, harness the
current of your blood flowing
in brittle rivers. You told me god

was closer to me than my jugular vein,
but I didn't know he would become
my own hangman.

You did sit me at the kitchen table when
I was ten and draw a diagram
of the reproductive system, fallopian tubes

like spaghetti in your unsteady scribble,
but you never taught me about that post-coital,
post-courage ache, about the coral marks laced

down my back in pink ribbons, a dishevelled
present left half-eaten in a wrapper
of bedsheets and semen.

You should have told me that they like
to make you scream so they can trace
the O of your mouth with their fingers,

that every sound convinces them
of their power, that sex is a power struggle,
that everything is a power struggle.

Why didn't you warn me, Mama?
Why didn't you tell me they like to get rough?

That their roughness
is a baby's head snapping back,
the crack of a glow stick, a slap?

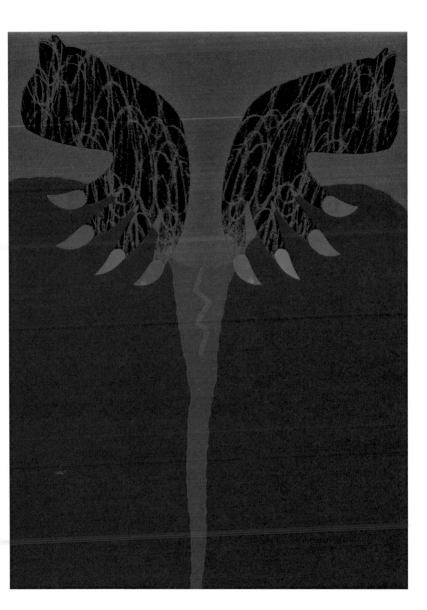

Loving them is like digging fish hooks
into my own palms,
self-inflicted stigmata.

Why didn't you tell me they would leave holes,
that there would be a void blistering in my chest?

You told me the angels came to the prophet,
lifted his heart from his breast, washed it with light.
Tell me, Mama, why won't they do the same for me?

Why didn't you tell me not to seek shelter
in men, show me the sanctuary I carried
all this time within myself?

I wish you'd told me
vulnerability was my power,
softness my greatest strength,

that you would be proud of me
if I could maintain kindness
in the face of devastation,

if I could keep calm while performing
an autopsy on myself,

hands steady as I lift my heart
from my own chest.

TAUTOLOGY

Life is a series of if-then statements:
iff I expect nothing—> I won't be disappointed
iff I go to a therapist —> I won't feel disjointed

iff I talk about it —> my body and brain will realign
iff I am vulnerable —> I'll consign you to the mausoleum of my
    mind
But it doesn't proof because our love wasn't logical.

I thought you meant it
when you said you loved me.
I reciprocated, modus ponens:

iff you love me —> I love you
^ you love me
∴ I must love you

But somehow the theorem got twisted
because when kisses turned to body pinned on
mattresses, purple marks on clavicles,

raspberry fields on bones,
I wondered if loving you meant I hated myself.
The more you told me about your scars,

the more scars I found on myself.
Iff you love me —> I love you

but you don't love me.

You can't love me. The words
you speak don't honour me, a text
every five minutes to check

up on me, comments about my clothing,
you act like you own me.
Everything I say tickles or titillates you

and you can't help it because I'm so damn cute,
especially when I'm dreaming.
I pretend to be asleep while you tower

over me in my little pink bed, pray
that you'll stop as you rob me thinking
I'll never know if something goes missing.

I know.

There's a six-foot hole inside me;
did you think I wouldn't notice?
A moment of silence, condolences

for the home that was transformed
into a tombstone.

> *But from my rotting body flowers shall grow
> and I am in them, and that is eternity.*

There's a lotus blooming from the grave inside me.
This is my opus:
I will use you as you have used me

but I will create something beautiful out of you.
Where you only knew how to seduce and abuse
I will make music.

I will heal hearts where you broke them;
where you choked throats I will breathe sweetness.
I'm not versed in the coldness of your killer

mathematics, but I'm versed in words.
Language that bars the hardness

of your gaze, soothes the wounds you
bequeathed my neck, cures

the cynic in me who wouldn't trust
for the longest time. I will repair
every cell that you infected and I'll be damned

if I won't let a man kiss my neck again
because the ghost of your fingers
still lingers there

❖

I am the proof that disproves your illogical love.

A RATIONALE FOR LIVING

Picking a crimson leaf bigger than my hand.
Ordering dessert before dinner.

The sound of champagne popping.
Scones with cream and jam.

The woman sitting on the table
in the bakery playing ukulele.

Buying croissants burned
on the bottom but big as my foot.

The flower shop with silk peonies
I thought were real. That black

velvet dress I bought on a whim
that skims my legs when I walk.

A bowl of cereal at 11pm. Peppermint cream
on my feet after a long day at work.

Kate laughing so hard milk spurts
out her nose. Bath bombs that smell

like blackcurrant. Blanket scarves so wide
they wrap around me twice.

Waiting for the light to change at the crosswalk.
Buying milk from the man

with the dimple piercing at the Co-op.
My sled tearing down winter hills, tears

squealing from my eyes. Brewing chai
in the pan, the way my father taught me.

Taking a train to the beach. Treading
heel-toe footprints. Climbing cliffs so tall

their jagged heads stroke heaven. The wind
petting little purple flowers,

roots like thin-boned fists digging into the soil.
Lights twinkling on the opposite shore.

The water's whispering, salt's drying crystal
on my lips. Dog running on the sand is a pinprick.

These are the things I would have missed
if I had jumped.

I would have missed
the call saying I got the job,

the tango of tannins peppering my tongue,
the crisp gin taste of the Spanish chef in my mouth.

My toes curl inside my boots.
I'll watch the leaves fall

and hear the Christmas songs come on too early.
I'll sit behind my house to watch the corn fields

yawn out gold. I'll hear
my mother call me in for tea.

These cheeks are flushed pink.
Blood is gushing through these blue threads.

This chest shouts for life, it beats,
it breathes.

FISH

I ain't waiting. I ain't waiting
for your texts anymore. I ain't
waiting for your permission,
your plate-smashing love –

I ain't waiting for love, period.
They say time heals all wounds
but it's been three years
and I'm not waiting for you

to leave anymore, I'm telling you
to get out.
I won't let the past reassert itself
when the women in my family

have waited four generations to
arrive. Amina married off
at fifteen, Nanijan babied and
pregnant again

at seventeen, Mother engaged
three months after she meets
the man who will cheat
on her twenty years later.

It's time to make that immigrant dream
mean something, to leave the men
behind until I birth a life that's
significant, a life that's all mine.

I just couldn't wait for this fledgling
girl to be pushed out the nest; I had to jump.
Fuck whether or not I knew how to fly;
I figured it out on the way down.

I propose a toast to the girl
who broke the cycle. I herald
the arrival of the family doctors,
lawyers, teachers, poets, talent

no longer stifled, women no longer
frightened of their excellence;
we keep a black dot behind the ear
to fight the nasr, no more evil eyes,

no more infanticide,
you won't marry us off, won't
bury us
before we're damn well ready.

When I was a baby, two Monet paintings
fell next to me while I was sleeping.
My parents rushed upstairs to find poppies
and water lilies skimming my unbroken body.

Mom said she knew then that god had plans for me.
With my toes kissing the frame of my own grave
I swear I will never be erased.
I will not let you take my capacity for love.

I won't let you ruin every man I will ever have,
won't become a marble statue,
Galatea in reverse, kiss of breath slurped
back up, marble arms clenching marble

chest holding marble air
in cold marble breast,
because what is it to be human if
you're not loved? If you don't love

easy as breathing? If you're not raw
tender   open   vulnerable
One day, I want to kiss someone
whose lips taste like a carnival, but

I won't wait for it
because last night I dreamed about fish.
Millions of them swimming giddy, oiled scales
gliding sunshine, scarlet, cobalt blue.

I looked it up in the dream dictionary
and it means I'm forgetting about you.
And I am. I'm tearing
out of this bruised body.

I'm clawing out of my own chest, I
am coming. My body has starved too long
for kindness, eaten itself.
Now, I am here to eat you.

FOR VICTOR

It's been fifteen months
and I finally feel clean.
Appreciating the green sprouting
from the brown clay of my skin,
I unfurl my arms, let the light in.

It pours into all the cracks that split
me into this fritzing
                fizzling
                      fragmented being.

I could have never foreseen this.

The shrubs of new life sprouting shyly
after a forest fire. The glassy sound
of silence following the screams
that were clashing
and jangling
and clamouring
in my head, the dissonance drilling
down spine
as I anticipated you
in the fingertips of every person
I touched.

But there's something about the sun
wiggling in after a night so long
that everything's been greyed.

Along my arms
there are furry flowers still clasped
in their blanket buds.

There are copper patina flakes of moss
cracked like mosaic tiles on my branches.
He tells me they're called *lichen.*

Eyelash-thin spiders spin webs
that filter sunlight like morning coffee –
how many things did I walk by every day
                              and not notice?

There are stick-legged sisters
in their school uniforms laughing
like twin twig bugs, brick-white
smiles on their brown faces.

There are old women on park benches
with hunchbacks and pink hair, old men
in flat caps whose thousand-yard stare
rests only a foot in front
of the crocuses which have snapped
up from the sleepy ground.

As I walk through town for the first time
in weeks, I buy roses from a street vendor.
They look like their edges have been dipped
in tea, parchment petals wrapped up

in brown paper as he hands them to me,
his forehead lines creased, guileless blue eyes
smiling bright enough to match the Devon sky.

A woman walks across the road in a yellow coat
and it's like a sun has grown legs
and decided to pace around for a while
just to find out what the view is like
from the ground.

At night, walking home, I watch two satellites swim
across the sky and I wonder how
my universe reoriented itself like this.

How swears
and blues
and booze
and bruises   dissipated

and I learned new cedar scent
                    messy head of mahogany hair
                    kindness and
                    honesty and
                    wobbly legs and
                    solace and
                    the promise of something fresh.

I crack open my windows to let it in.
Feel the pink light singeing my hair, singing
through my skin.
I lean out and drink it in.

Something in that sky is calling out
to my heart and I am finally able to answer

                    I am here.

I want to be that girl kissing her boyfriend smack
in the middle of the street, just to prove I have it in me.

Because I do still have it in me.

Still have the capacity to love.
Still have the capacity to trust.
Still have the capacity to be unashamed
of the person I am with.

He asks me: how do you know
when you're in love?

I might have forgotten
but I can't wait to remember.

ACKNOWLEDGEMENTS

Living by the quote 'I am a part of all that I have met', thank you to everyone with whom I have crossed paths. You have without a doubt influenced this book in some way.

Thank you, Mom – you've heard the first draft of every poem in this book, and I know it wasn't always easy.

Thank you, Victor – for being gentle and for being patient. Your kindness is an unceasing gift.

Thank you to all of the poets I have met and worked with for teaching me your craft, for sharing, and for giving me the courage to share too.

I am especially grateful to the two artists whose work features in this collection. Renee M Kumar designed the cover art – you can find more of her work at www.reneekumar.com. Sophie Leary created the art you see nestled in between the poetry – you can find more of her work at www.babybesso.com.